_____

The Lion and the Mouse
© Thomas-Bo Huusmann
Published by Huusmann Media
illustrated by: Thomas-Bo Huusmann
ISBN: 978-87-995724-0-3

More books by author:

Fox and the Crow
Lazy Elf
Rain on a sunny day
Pippa Filippa and The Pirate Frog

Publisher Address:
Huusmann Media
Ceres Allé 1, 8000 Aarhus, Denmark
phone: +45 25 73 50 59
e-mail: contact@huusmann.com
www.huusmann.com

THE LION AND THE MOUSE

Published by Huusmann Media

Once when a Lion was asleep,
a little mouse was jumping
up and down upon him

This soon wakened the Lion,
who placed his big paw upon
the Mouse

What a tiny little annoying thing, to wake such a mighty king from his beauty sleep, the Lion thought

...and the Lion opened his big jaws to swallow the little Mouse. "Pardon, O king," cried the Mouse

"oh forgive me, I shall never forget it. Who knows maybe one day I will be able to do you a turn?" added the Mouse

The Lion was so tickled at the Idea of the Mouse being able to help him...

... That he lifted up his paw
and let the Mouse go. "Thank you,
dear King of beasts. You will not
regret it" repeated the Mouse

In the forest where the Lion and the Mouse had their homes, lived a Hunter, who loved setting up traps to catch animals

Then one day the Lion was
on a royal stroll in the forest
when suddenly...

BANG..WOOSH..SNAP and the Lion was caught in the Hunter's trap.

The Hunter who desired to carry him alive to the Zoo, tied the Lion to a tree

Then the Hunter went in search of a Wagon to carry the Lion.

The little Mouse happened to pass by, and seeing the sad predicament the Lion was in...

...He went down to the Lion and said "Was I not right?"

Then gnawed away the rope
and freed the King of Beasts

Now freed, The Lion smiled to the Mouse and together they hurried deep into the forest.

It is true, when said:
Little friends may prove great friends.

THE END

Big thanks to:

Aima R. Jasper, Birgit Huusmann

Claus Hansson, Daniel Sim,

Jan Rybka, Kasper F. Mikkelsen,

Mark Oftedal, Sirid G. Vejrum,

Tod Polson, Ture S. Poulsen

Thanks to all who I interupted with my many thoughts, in the making of this book!

Too bad it had to end. :-)

www.ingramcontent.com/pod-product-compliance
Lightning Source LLC
Chambersburg PA
CBHW041235040426
42444CB00002B/166